EXPLORING WORLD CULTURES

Mexico

Ruth Bjorklund

Cavendish
Square

New York

Published in 2016 by Cavendish Square Publishing, LLC
243 5th Avenue, Suite 136, New York, NY 10016

Website: cavendishsq.com

This publication represents the opinions and views of the author based on his or her personal experience, knowledge, and research. The information in this book serves as a general guide only. The author and publisher have used their best efforts in preparing this book and disclaim liability rising directly or indirectly from the use and application of this book.

CPSIA Compliance Information: Batch #WS15CSQ

All websites were available and accurate when this book was sent to press.

Cataloging-in-Publication Data

Bjorklund, Ruth.
Mexico / by Ruth Bjorklund.
p. cm. — (Exploring world cultures)
Includes index.
ISBN 978-1-50260-589-4 (hardcover) ISBN 978-1-50260-588-7 (paperback)
ISBN 978-1-5026-0590-0 (ebook)
1. Mexico — Juvenile literature. I. Bjorklund, Ruth. II. Title.
F1208.5 B56 2016
972—d23

Editorial Director: David McNamara
Editor: Kristen Susienka
Copy Editor: Cynthia Roby
Art Director: Jeffrey Talbot
Designer: Joseph Macri
Senior Production Manager: Jennifer Ryder-Talbot
Production Editor: Renni Johnson
Photo Research: J8 Media

Printed in the United States of America

Contents

Mexico is a special country. It has jungles, deserts, volcanoes, ocean beaches, big cities, and small villages. A wide variety of plants, such as palm trees and desert cactus, grow there. Many different animals, such as butterflies, iguanas, and jaguars, live there, too.

Mexico has a fascinating history. In early times, it was the home of great civilizations, including the Mayan and the Aztec people. These people could read and write, studied the stars, and made tools and decorations from silver and gold. Later, Spanish explorers brought new beliefs and languages to them.

These girls in colorful costumes are performing a traditional Mexican dance.

The climate is warm and sunny, and people spend most of their time outdoors. Mexicans are friendly people. They are close to their families and enjoy many lively celebrations each year. Mexico is a great place to live in and visit.

Geography

Mexico is in North America. It is south of the United States. It has an amazing variety of plants, animals, and land formations.

Mexico has two large mountain ranges and many volcanoes. Between the mountains is the Valley of Mexico. Most of the farmland and people are in this region.

Be Aware

Mexico experiences many hurricanes, earthquakes, tsunamis, and volcanic eruptions.

Northern Mexico and the Baja California **peninsula** are deserts where cacti grow. Palm trees line the beaches along the Pacific Ocean and the Gulf of Mexico. Rain forests cover the Yucatán

Peninsula and southern Mexico. Deserts and beaches are hot, but temperatures are cooler in the mountains.

Mexico is a large country below the United States.

Bears, deer, and coyotes live in Mexico's forests. Many plants, such as flowers, bananas, and coconuts, are found in the rain forests. You can see lots of colorful birds and butterflies there, too.

Each year, gray whales swim from Alaska to Mexico to raise their babies.

Over thousands of years, many groups came to live in Mexico. The earliest Mexicans were farmers. Some groups were stone carvers. Others built pyramids and big cities.

Hernándo Cortés was one of the first explorers of Mexico.

In 1519, a Spanish army led by Hernándo Cortés took over Mexico. They forced people to work in gold mines and on farms. Native Mexicans suffered for three centuries under Spanish rule before

The Aztecs

The most ancient groups to live in Mexico were the Aztecs and the Maya. They built temples and cities.

they fought back. In 1861, Spain gave Mexico its independence.

New Mexican leaders passed laws giving poor farmers their own land. Years later, Mexicans fought another war called the Mexican Revolution. Afterwards, the Mexican government wrote a **constitution** giving people more rights.

FACT!

Emiliano Zapata was a hero in the Mexican Revolution. His battle cry was "Land and Liberty!"

The flag of Mexico

Mexico is known officially as the United Mexican States. There are thirty-one states and a special area surrounding the capital, Mexico City. The Constitution of Mexico created three **branches** of government: the executive, legislative, and judicial.

Mexico once ruled Texas, California, Nevada, Utah, and parts of Arizona, New Mexico, Wyoming, and Colorado.

The president is the head of the executive branch. The legislative branch is called the Congress of the Union. Its members make the laws. It has two parts: the Senate and the Chamber of Deputies. The judicial branch is led by the Supreme Court of Justice.

Mexico City is one of the largest cities in the world. The Spanish built it on top of the ancient city Tenochtitlán. Mexico City is very modern, but pyramids and Aztec ruins are close by.

FACT!

The first native Mexican president was Benito Juarez.

Mexican people have many professions. Some are farmers. They grow corn, tomatoes, and peppers. Many farmers sell vegetables to the United States. Other people work in cities as teachers, businesspeople,

Mexican farm families work together.

lawyers, or factory workers. Many countries have factories in Mexico. Some Mexican-made products are clothing, shoes, furniture, and cars.

In the past, most people lived in the countryside, but now many people live and work in cities.

Mexico is a beautiful country to visit. Many people visit each year. Tourists from around the world travel there to see Mexico's beaches and historic places.

A Good Place to Visit

Many people from the United States visit Mexico. In 2013, twenty million people from the United States went there on vacation.

The Pyramid of the Moon

Dirty air, called smog, often hangs over Mexico City.

Mexico has many waterfalls, beaches, lakes, and streams. However, areas of Mexico are growing and causing problems for the environment.

There is a lot of pollution in Mexico. Trucks and cars make the air dirty. People use a lot of water and energy. In the country, farmers also use

14

a lot of water. Trees are cut to create farms. Many lakes and streams are being fished in too much. Many animals suffer.

FACT!

People put fences around the beaches where sea turtles lay their eggs to protect them.

The country has plans to save the environment. More people use solar, wind, or water power for their homes and businesses. In cities, more people ride bicycles and drive cars that pollute less.

Keeping Pollution Close

The exhaust from cars and trucks makes Mexico City's air thick and gray. The mountains that surround the city make it difficult for the dirty air to leave the area.

Today many different groups of people call Mexico home. About 60 percent are of mixed **ethnicities**. Thirty percent are native Mexicans and 9 percent are

Most Mexican people share a mixed heritage of Spanish and Native Mexic

white. People of African, Arab, or Asian descent make up 1 percent.

There are more than fifty different native Mexican groups in the country. The two largest groups are the Maya and the Nahua, who are relatives of the Aztec people.

Other Cultures

Many Mayan, Nahua, and other Native people live in faraway villages and follow ancient customs and traditional ways of life.

People honor their family's **heritage**. There are celebrations many times during the year. Mexican families spend a lot of time together, enjoying each other's company.

Even though the people of Mexico are different, they are all proud to be Mexican.

FACT!

Mexico has a population of just under 123 million people. Nearly 22 million live in Mexico City.

Mexican families celebrate special events and holidays together.

Family in Mexico is important. Often, relatives live close to each other. Children learn good manners and to show respect for elders. Traditionally, men are in charge of the family while women take care of the children. This is changing in Mexico.

Life for Mexicans is different depending on where they live. Many people in cities have cell phones and computers. Many families in the country have TV. Some families live on very little. Some families have a lot.

All children ages six to fifteen attend school. More young people in cities go to high school than those living in villages. Big cities have colleges and universities.

Education First

The Aztecs were one of the first societies to educate all children.

Religion

When the Spanish arrived in Mexico, they brought their religion with them. The Spanish believed in **Catholicism**. Today, 90 percent of Mexicans are Catholic. Other religions, such as Native religions, Islam, Mormonism, and

Many Catholic churches in Mexi are built in the Spanish style.

El Día de los Muertos

El día de los muertos, meaning the Day of the Dead, is celebrated on November 1. People honor their ancestors by visiting graves. They leave flowers and food.

Protestantism, are also common. Some people do not follow a religion. Before Catholicism, ancient people worshipped many gods. People prayed for good crops and health.

Our Lady of Guadalupe

Catholics celebrate special people, called saints. These celebrations are called feast days. The Feast Day of Our Lady of Guadalupe, the "mother" of Mexico, is very important. Other religious holidays include Christmas, Easter, and the Day of the Dead.

FACT!

About 6 percent of Mexicans are of the Protestant faith.

Language

Students speak and write Spanish in school, but many also study Native languages.

Spanish is the main language of Mexico. It is used in classrooms and official documents. But it is not the only language. The Mexican government wants people to keep the languages spoken by Native groups alive, too.

Today there are sixty-two Native languages spoken in Mexico. Nearly 8 percent of Mexicans

Spanish Speakers

Mexico has more Spanish-speaking people than any other country in the world.

speak a Native language as well as Spanish. In school, many people also learn American English. It is important to learn English to communicate with a large part of the world.

Many words used in Mexico have come from different Native languages and American English. "Chili," "tomato," and "chocolate" come from the Nahuatl language. The words "Internet" and "text" come from American English.

FACT!

Nearly 98 percent of Mexican people aged fifteen to twenty-five can read and write.

Arts and Festivals

Mexicans enjoy many arts, crafts, and festivals. Since ancient times, they have made clothes, jewelry, pots, baskets, and rugs. People continue these traditions today.

A traditional mariachi band

Special Celebrations

Independence Day and **Cinco de Mayo** are patriotic Mexican celebrations. There are speeches, parades, fireworks, and chants of "¡Viva Mexico!" ("Long live Mexico!")

Art museums display many Mexican sculptures and paintings. Diego Rivera was a popular artist who painted murals—large paintings on walls. His wife, Frida Kahlo, is famous for her self-portraits and scenes from everyday life.

Mexican parties are called fiestas. Many fiestas have music played at them. Mexican music is famous for guitars, small bands called mariachis, and sad songs called *ranchera* music. People also listen and dance to popular, classical, and folk music.

FACT!

Every year, girls who turn fifteen have a *quinciñera*. This is a big party that celebrates a girl growing up.

Mexican people work hard. When they have time for themselves, they enjoy fun and games.

Mexico's national soccer team

Soccer, called *fútbol*, is the country's favorite sport. Many children and young adults play soccer during their free time. Mexicans are great fans. When the national team plays in an international soccer tournament, everyone

Mexico City's bullfighting ring, La Monumental, can hold forty thousand people. It is the largest bullfighting ring in the world.

watches. Everyone celebrates when the team wins. They wave flags, honk horns, and cheer.

The Spanish brought bullfighting to Mexico.

Baseball, called *béisbol*, is another favorite pastime. There are many local teams and sixteen professional teams that play during the summer.

Semana Santa

Semana Santa (Holy Week) is the week before Easter and a big vacation time for all.

Other sports are swimming, hiking, fishing, golf, and tennis. Boxing, wrestling, and bullfighting are also popular.

Tortillas are part of nearly every Mexican meal.

Mexican food is a blend of Native and Spanish foods. Early Mexicans ate corn, squash, beans, and peppers. The Spanish introduced meat and wheat flour. Foods from native plants are chocolate, peanuts, and vanilla.

Breakfast is usually small. Pastry, coffee, and juices are served. Most people eat a big meal late in the afternoon and a light meal at night.

Olé Mole

A special native dish is *mole* (MO-lay), a sauce for meat made from peanuts, chilies, and chocolate.

Typical foods are beans, rice, meat, fish, and avocados. Mexicans flavor food with peppers, called chilies, and sauces, called salsas. Meals include a flatbread called a tortilla.

Special treats such as *tamales*, a mixture of meat and dough roasted in corn husks, and *empanadas*, a meat-filled pastry, are served at fiestas. Fancy decorated cakes are fun to eat.

FACT!

Mexicans eat a prickly cactus called *nopale* (no-PAH-lay). Cooks must remove its tiny thorns.

Glossary

branches Parts of a government.

Catholicism A religion that believes that Jesus Christ is the Messiah and is governed by the pope.

Cinco de Mayo A Mexican holiday that celebrates a battle won on the fifth of May.

constitution A document that gives a country laws to follow.

ethnicities Social groups that have a common national or cultural tradition.

heritage Anything from the past that has been handed down through generations.

peninsula A body of land that is surrounded on three sides by water.

Find Out More

Books

McManus, Lori. *Mexican Culture*. Chicago: Heinemann, 2013.

Somerville, Barbara. *It's Cool To Learn About Mexico*. Ann Arbor, MI: Cherry Lake Publishing, 2011.

Websites

Mysterious Mayas and Awesome Aztecs

mayas.mrdonn.org and aztecs.mrdonn.org

TIME for Kids: Mexico

www.timeforkids.com/destination/mexico

Video

Mexican Folk Dance Spectacle

www.youtube.com/watch?v=t8w0ZalwroQ

Watch traditional Mexican dancing.

Index

About the Author

Ruth Bjorklund lives on an island near Seattle, Washington. She has written more than forty books for young people. Mexico is one of her family's favorite places to visit.

5

www.carameltree.com